SKETCHES OF ETON

SKETCHES OF ETON

ETCHINGS & VIGNETTES

by

RICHARD S. CHATTOCK

AND

DESCRIPTIVE NOTES
BY
W. WIGHTMAN WOOD

Republised S.R. Publishers Ltd., 1971
First published London, 1874

Lane Walk.

SKETCHES OF ETON.

ETCHINGS AND VIGNETTES

BY

RICHARD S. CHATTOCK,

AND

DESCRIPTIVE NOTES

BY

W. WIGHTMAN WOOD,

Of the Inner Temple,
An Ex-Captain of the Oppidans.

SEELEY, JACKSON, AND HALLIDAY, FLEET STREET.
LONDON, MDCCCLXXIV.

PREFACE.

Eton attracts such deep feelings of attachment from all who have received an education there, and so much attention from the general public, that we venture to think these "Sketches," drawn and written, may be found to some extent to supply a want that is felt by Etonians of a memento, and by other persons of an account, of this engrossing locality ; and that whatever apologies are required for the manner of its execution, none are necessary for the intention of this design. The object of both author and artist has been to awaken pleasing recollections in old Etonians, and at the same time to convey a fair idea of the place to strangers.

As some of our readers may not be conversant with the art and mystery of Etching, it will not perhaps be thought out of place if we give a short description of the process, and indicate some of the advantages which have led to its adoption for the chief subjects of the following series. And first let us notice, in order to dissipate it, an impression which is sometimes found to prevail that "etching" is the same thing as drawing with pen and ink. One frequently hears of "etchings" being done by amateurs which prove on inspection to be simply drawings, more or less elaborate, executed with a fine pointed pen upon paper. But whatever title it may be allowable to apply to such a drawing, it is clearly incorrect to style it an "etching," for the art of Etching (so called from the German *etzen* " to eat ") consists essentially in the *erosion* of lines upon a metal or other surface by means of *aqua fortis*. In order to effect this the plate is in the first instance protected with an extremely thin coating of some material— such as resin, wax, or asphaltum—which is capable of resisting the action of the *aqua fortis*, and the design is then traced upon the metal through the coating, or "etching-ground" as it is called, by means of a stout needle point. The plate is then immersed in a bath of *aqua fortis*, which attacks those portions from which the "ground" has been removed by the needle, eating out the metal to a depth proportionate to the length of its exposure, the lines which are intended to be faint being exposed to the eroding action for a short period only, while the heavier lines are allowed to remain longer.

The artist's work being thus traced upon the plate by his own hand, exhibits of necessity a more direct and unerring expression of his intention than can be obtained by any process requiring the intervention of the engraver—and the freedom of manipulation resulting from the fact that the tracing is effected with a polished metal point gliding unconstrainedly over a polished metal surface is such as to distinguish, to its manifest advantage, the etched line from that executed by the burin of the engraver which, being with labour ploughed out of the metal, necessarily lacks the perfect spontaneity of the other.

But there is another point in which etching has a strength of its own. In some subjects passages occur which it is desirable to treat with the richness of quality seen in *mezzotinto* engraving. For this purpose recourse is had, after the "biting" is completed, to a process known to etchers and engravers as "dry-pointing," consisting in working delicately over the portion to be enriched with the well-sharpened point of the etching needle—engraving upon it, in fact, a multitude of lines or scratches. Along the side of each of these lines the needle turns up a tiny ridge of metal known technically as the "bur"—just as a ploughshare turns up the soil along the furrow. To the line engraver, whose object is to obtain the cleanest possible line, this "bur" is hateful, as it catches the ink when the plate is wiped for printing, and produces what appears in his work as a dirty mark ; and he is at great pains to scrape it off, and leave the dry-point line pure and simple. The etcher, however, does not so regard it, for he finds that, judiciously employed, the "bur" is invaluable for the soft velvety richness which it imparts to his work, and which no other means enable him to produce. In the following series much use has been made of it in the reflections of water in the plates of "*Sixth Form Bench*," "the *Brocas*," and "*Surly Hall*," in the foreground of "the *Thames at Oakley*," and to enrich the deep shadows in the plates generally.

The vignettes printed with the text are produced by a new process, which the inventor, Mr. Alfred Dawson, a son of the well-known painter, calls "*Typographic Etching*." The etched line, in this process, instead of being bitten into the plate, is made to stand up in relief, and the illustration can be printed with letterpress, like a woodcut.

W. W. W.
R. S. C.

London, Dec., 1873.

LIST OF THE ETCHINGS.

FROM SALT HILL.

SKETCHES OF ETON.

I.

GENERAL VIEW OF ETON COLLEGE.

"THE Kynge's College of our Blessed Ladye of Etone, besyde Windesore," is the full style and title of the renowned public school universally known in the present day as plain "Eton." It was founded by the unfortunate King Henry VI., in 1440, the conveyance of the advowson of Eton to the King bearing date "Windsor, Sept. 12, 19 Henry VI.," and the first charter from the King to the College following upon Oct. 11 in the same year. For some little time, however, either the institution existed only upon paper, or the Collegiate Body must have boarded out, for the brick-and-mortar foundation resulting in the imposing block of buildings which is the subject of our etching taken from the River, was not commenced until July 1441, and a considerable period must have elapsed before its completion, as it was certainly not run up by the contractors of the period with the rapidity which their successors in the Victorian era are wont to exhibit.

No happier site for his foundation could possibly have been selected by the King. The propinquity of Royal Windsor, the charms of the Thames, and the facility of communication with the metropolis, combine to render Eton the most convenient and agreeable locality in the country for a great upper-class school; and it is not too much to say, that its fortunate situation has done more than even its noble buildings and rich endowments, towards promoting the extension of the royal foundation, and making it —or rather engrafting upon it—the foremost public school in the land. Henry VI. put his hand pretty deeply into his own, or other people's, pockets when endowing his new establishment; and though his successful rival Edward IV., with more appreciation of the value than the piety of his unfortunate predecessor's munificent grant, threatened total disendowment, and did in fact dispossess the College of part of its wealth, the bulk was saved, principally through the exertions of William of Waynflete (afterwards Bishop of Winchester), who, having been the first Head Master, was Provost at the time of the attempted spoliation. The annual income derived from the College property at the present day is stated to be upwards of £20,000; but for further information on the subject we must refer inquirers to the Provost and Fellows, unless, indeed, the new "Governing Body" have got at the secret and are willing to disclose it: all that *we* can say about it, is that, whatever the amount may be, it will be greatly enhanced when the pernicious system, common to capitular bodies, of renewing leases upon lives on payment of fines no longer affects the estates. As the result of recent legislation and the Ecclesiastical Commission the "lives" are now allowed to die out without renewal, and with the last of them this system of leasing will expire as far as Eton College property is concerned. We must not omit to mention that the College was dedicated by its pious founder not only to the Blessed Virgin, but also to St. Nicholas, who is the patron saint of scholars *in statu pupillari*, and—it must be added—of thieves, though it is but reasonable to suppose that this latter connection is set up solely by the thieves and is indignantly repudiated by the saint. It is on account of this double dedication that the 2nd of February, the 25th of March, and the 6th of December (St. Nicholas' day) are termed "Founder's Days" at Eton, and are duly observed by the College authorities; the only extant ceremony connected with the observance consisting, of course, in a big dinner. The original College buildings were comprised in the two quadrangles known as "the School Yard" and "the Cloisters," and (with the exception of "the Upper School" and some boarding-houses for Oppidans) no extension of this ample accommodation was found

The College from the River
H.J.C. 1873

necessary until within the last thirty years, since which time additional buildings of various kinds have sprung up in great profusion—notably the "New Buildings" for Collegers in Weston's Yard and the "New Schools," to say nothing of numerous Masters' Houses on a large scale. Nevertheless the present accommodation, in proportion to the numbers for whom it is provided, appears small when contrasted with the space placed at the disposal of the mere handful of which the College originally consisted.

Henry the Sixth's first foundation was for a Provost, ten Priests, a Master, four Clerks, six Choristers, twenty-five "poor grammar scholars," and twenty-five "poor men" (Bedesmen) "to pray for the King." A few years later he increased the number of scholars to seventy, added an Usher (or Lower Master), and ten Chaplains, and more than doubled the strength of the choir; at the same time, however, knocking off a dozen Bedesmen. Edward the Fourth's raid, and, at a later period, the Reformation effected some changes in this list. The ten "Priests" were converted into seven "Fellows;" the ten Chaplains were "reduced," and three "Conducts"* (as the Curates are termed) substituted; the choir was borrowed instead of kept at home; and the remaining "poor men" and their prayers disappeared altogether—having been handed over, we suppose, to the Poor Law Guardians as soon as that remarkable body came into existence, at which period it is possible that the "prayers for the King" were deemed a sufficient "labour test." Thus modified, the Collegiate Body—properly so called—has continued the same to the present time, with the addition only of ten "old women," who at some period were brought into the establishment to satisfy the conscientious scruples of the Fellows with regard to the extermination of the "poor men," and who do not seem to have been considered at all out of place. All the old foundation Fellowships are now, however, moribund, existing

---

* Conductitii—hired.

only during the lives of their present holders ; but the name will be maintained, as the new Governing Body, of whom we have yet to speak, have been pleased to constitute themselves " Fellows."

The primary duty of the Head and Lower Masters has always been the education of the seventy King's Scholars or "Collegers" (as they are more usually called), but at an early period they commenced the practice of taking private pupils, who came to Eton for the purpose, and boarded at houses in the town. Hence arose the " Oppidans,"* and " Dames," the latter being strong-minded ladies of a certain age, who were authorized by the Head Master to provide young gentlemen seeking the advantages of an Eton education with board and lodging. The Oppidans, though scarcely recognised by the Collegiate Body, like the Israelites in Egypt, multiplied exceedingly; and in the middle of the last century there were as many as 520 of them at the School ; that, however, appears to have been an abnormal state of things, due to the popularity of the Head Master of the day, Dr. Bernard; and in the early years of the present century the number of Oppidans ranged from 350 to 470. From 1812 to 1852 the School fluctuated considerably: during that period the minimum, including Collegers, was 444 in 1836, and the maximum was 777 in 1846. In 1853 the sum-total was 600, and since then there has been a continuous increase. Ten years ago the School numbered 830, and now it contains 930, and "the cry is still ' They come.' " If the tide rises much higher, the place will be destroyed, and yet it is a difficult matter for the authorities to stem it, especially as the increase is not disproportioned to that of the wealth and population of the country. The introduction of the Oppidans necessarily led to a staff of Assistants being required by the Head Master to aid in their instruction and discipline. These Assistant Masters soon, of course, came to share with the Dames the remunerative privilege of keeping boarding-houses ; and, as every boy in the school is

---

* Oppidani—townsmen.

obliged to be placed under the special supervision of one of the Masters, who is thereupon called his "tutor," and directs his classical studies, the houses of the Masters who take pupils are called "Tutors' Houses," in contradistinction to the "Dames' Houses," under which latter term is now included not only the establishments presided over by elderly ladies, as before mentioned, very few of which still exist, but also the houses under the control of Mathematical* and Extra Masters; in short, all boarding-houses other than those in the hands of "Tutors." The word "Dame," then, in the language of modern Eton, is both masculine and feminine; but nevertheless, it must be observed that the husband of a Dame *in her own right* is termed a "Dom"†—a functionary, by the way, who is as completely shelved in an Eton boarding-house as is the consort of a Queen-regnant in the British constitution. There has never been any numerical superfluity in the educational staff at Eton. In 1812 there were five Assistant Masters in the Upper School, and three in the Lower School; and in addition to these there were five "Extra Masters," one of whom taught writing, and another dancing. In 1863 there were seventeen Assistant Masters in the Upper School, four in the Lower School, eight in the Mathematical School, and six for Extra subjects—viz., French, German, Italian, Drawing, Fencing, and Dancing. At the present time there are twenty-eight Classical Assistants (the division into Upper and Lower Schools having been abolished), and ten Mathematical; there are also eight Masters for subjects which were formerly, but are now no longer, termed "Extras," three of whom are for French, and the remainder for Chemistry, German, Italian, Drawing, and Music respectively. With regard to boarding accommodation, there are, in addition to the "College" proper, twenty-eight Houses, of which eighteen are in the hands of Tutors, and the remainder are Dames' Houses—terms already explained.

---

* One Mathematical Master is now, by a recent innovation, a "tutor."

† Dominie.

Two only of the Dames are at this time ladies; two others are gentlemen who take no part in teaching, and the other six are Mathematical, French, or Drawing Masters. The Head Master, according to immemorial usage, takes neither pupils nor boarders; he has enough to do without the former, and is sufficiently remunerated without the latter. We say "sufficiently remunerated," because it is generally understood that the Lower Master and senior Assistant Masters are indirectly rewarded by the profits of a boarding-house for their inadequately paid services as teachers. Much attention has lately been called to this subject; but, after all, a similar anomaly exists in most professions; and it is not a little remarkable that at the present time, out of the eleven Assistant Masters who are senior by residence, only five have got "Houses," the other six having resigned theirs, after holding them for several years. Whether they have made their fortunes, or found that "the game was not worth the candle," is a question we must leave others to investigate.

During the last few years Eton has gone through the most eventful period of its existence, having, in common with most other ancient institutions, been subjected to a searching inquiry, and a large measure of reform, to the ultimate results of which, however, in this instance, we are not inclined to attach much importance one way or the other. In 1861 a Royal Commission was appointed to inquire into the revenues, administration, and course of studies at Eton and the eight other principal public schools respectively. The Commissioners took a large amount of evidence, documentary and oral, and presented their report in February, 1864. In it they made thirty-two general recommendations, and sixty-four upon Eton in particular. By far the most important matter as regards Eton that has resulted from their labours, is the creation of a new "Governing Body." The government of "the College" was in the hands of the Provost and Fellows; that of "the School" was vested in the Head Master subject to the control of the Provost, who, in practice, acted with the advice of the Fellows. The Commissioners reported that the Provost and

Romney Lock
P.J.L. 1873

Fellows were not well adapted for the exercise of their powers; that the election of the Head Master should be entrusted to a wider body, and one less amenable to local and personal influences; and that "it had not been beneficial to Eton that its education and discipline had been exclusively controlled by a small number of retired Masters, who could not but have some bias against any serious change in the system under which their own lives had been passed, and with the practical working of which they had ceased to be familiar." They therefore desired to see the Governing Body "include men conversant with the world, with the requirements of active life, and with the progress of literature and science." The Commissioners, it is presumed, have had their desire; though not quite in the form they recommended, which was an enlargement merely of the existing Body; for the Act of Parliament which was passed in 1868, as the sequel of the Report, goes beyond it in this particular, and creates an entirely new Governing Body, springing from very miscellaneous sources, and not necessarily including any of the Fellows of the old Foundation. THE NEW GOVERNING BODY OF ETON SCHOOL is thus constituted :—

THE PROVOST OF ETON, Chairman, *Ex Officio*.

THE PROVOST OF KING'S COLLEGE, CAMBRIDGE, *Ex Officio*.

THE VERY REV. R. SCOTT, D.D., Dean of Rochester. Nominated by the University of Oxford.

THE REV. W. H. THOMPSON, D.D., Master of Trinity College, Cambridge. Nominated by the University of Cambridge.

PROFESSOR G. G. STOKES. Nominated by the Royal Society.

G. K. RICKARDS, ESQ. Nominated by the Lord Chief Justice of England.

JOHN HIBBERT, ESQ. Nominated by the Masters.

RT. HON. S. H. WALPOLE, LL.D., Q.C., M.P.

THE REV. W. A. CARTER.

LORD LYTTELTON, LL.D.

THE EARL OF MORLEY.

All the members of this Board who were not already on the

Foundation, have been constituted " Fellows " of the College, by virtue of the new Statutes which they made and published in August, 1871, but no emoluments or obligatory residence are attached to their offices.

Our etching of " The College from the River " is taken from the right bank of the main stream, near Windsor (or Romney) Lock, of which we also give a sketch. No more general view of the

> " Spires and antique towers
> That crown the wat'ry glade "

can be obtained from any point ; therefore it naturally takes the first place in our text. Nevertheless, it is probably the last aspect of Eton that meets the eyes of the great majority of Etonians; for there is no approach to the College on this side by road, and the river in the foreground having just tumbled over Windsor Weir, affords no passage for boats, which are compelled to go through a deep lock-cut that shuts out all prospect beyond its own banks. It is in truth the back of the College that we are now looking at. This charming river frontage forms the East side of The Cloisters, and is divided into three or four residences for as many of the Fellows. The strip of grass land between their gardens and the river is an island known as " Fellows' Eyot," being separated from the main land by a narrow back-water. The twin turrets of the Clock Tower stand up boldly in the centre of our picture, but only to be dwarfed by their more eminent neighbours on the stately Chapel; while a singularly plain and lofty boarding-house is somewhat of an eyesore on the left of the scene; and the " Playing Fields" are just shut out on the right. The lower part of Fellows' Eyot and the junction of the back-water with the main stream are depicted in our etching of " Sixth Form Bench," a delightful spot in the " Playing Fields " to which we shall again recur.

II.

COLLEGE BUILDINGS.

NINETY-NINE out of every hundred visitors to Eton College approach it by way of Windsor Bridge, which is unfortunate in so far as they lose a particularly fine view of the place from the

WINDSOR BRIDGE.

opposite entrance by way of the Slough Road.   Emerging from the long narrow street of Eton on to the bridge over " Barnes' Pool " (presumably so called from its propinquity to the shop of a worthy confectioner of that name who drives a boisterous trade in superfluous food), the " new boy " suddenly finds himself " in

C

College," though there is very little chance that he will recognise his arrival as a *fait accompli* until he gets to the commencement of the low wall which, for about two hundred yards, separates the public high road from that part of the College property presumptuously entitled THE LONG WALK, upon the *lucus a non lucendo* principle, and fortunately, therefore, without any chance of being confounded with a certain other "Long Walk" not a hundred miles off. Having reached this spot he would look upon the subject of our frontispiece, and the veriest tyro would have no difficulty in satisfying himself that he had undoubtedly arrived at his destination. He would not, however, we feel sure, indulge himself at that early period of his Etonian career with more than a very cursory survey of the external form of his Alma Mater; and so far from asking any questions, his time would be fully occupied in answering the constant interrogatory put to him by small boys who had the advantage of him in seniority by "a half" or two—"What's your name and whose your Tutor?"

The low wall which we have alluded to, and of which a small portion figures in the foreground of our frontispiece, is worthy of more than a passing notice. This wall is quite an institution at Eton, and plays an important part in the domestic economy of the place. It is the favourite lounge of the "Lower Boy," and the regular place of business of a unique class of *al fresco* traders that ministers to his wants. A considerable trade is done across that wall, the staple commodities consisting not only of "sock" (the Etonian term for light and unnecessary refreshments, such as fruit, sweets, and oysters, the latter, by-the-bye, being in season on the wall in the hot months, and esteemed in proportion to their magnitude), but also of bats, balls, flowers, birds, dormice, and such like. The "men on the wall," as these purveyors are termed, are for the most part, from long association with the place, characters well known to all Etonians. Of such none has arisen equal to a remarkable individual whose soubriquet "Spankie" must be familiar to every Etonian in the country over ten years' standing. His trade was humble enough,

not extending beyond the sale of apples, and buns stuffed with
jam, his stock-in-trade consisting of a basket on one arm
and a tin on the other. But Spankie was a veritable Nestor,
with recollections of three generations of men, and a marvellous
memory for names and faces. His young customers were
frequently astonished to find how much more he knew of their
family history than they did themselves, and there was a general
belief that he could name straight off and give the pedigree of
any Etonian, old or young. Had he been located at Stonyhurst
instead of Eton, he might have been safely entrusted with the
decision of the Tichborne Case! There is, however, a slight
anachronism in that statement, for Spankie retired into private
life about ten years ago, and was gathered to his fathers not long
afterwards. Many other names of "wall characters" will occur
to the writer's contemporaries. There was "Picky" Powell, the
"Eton prize-fighter," who, having once defeated in battle one
Billy Warner, the champion of Harrow, ever afterwards traded
upon this questionable reputation, and constantly repeated the
performance in pantomime to an admiring circle of small
Etonians. Then there were Brian and Levi in Spankie's way of
business, and Joby *père*, who sold bats, and Joby *fils*, who
inflated footballs, and others *ejusdem generis;* and last but not
least was the old lady who sat in all weathers at the School Yard
Gate, and supplied Lower School boys with sweets and dormice.
She has outlived all her customers, for on our last visit to Eton
we found the Lower School extinct, and "missus" alive and well.
We hope that the Fourth Form are no longer above dealing with
her, and we are surprised to hear that her "vested interest" in
the Lower School was not respected upon its disestablishment.
Surely, according to modern ideas on the subject, she has a strong
claim to compensation, and we recommend the Governing Body
to settle it, or we shall probably hear of the old lady's grievance
in Parliament. She could no doubt obtain influential support, as
there must be many members in both Houses who have been
"under obligations" to her! The wall which has caused our

latest digression is the boundary-line of the original College. All the old buildings are within it. Those which come into our frontispiece are the north-west corner of the Chapel, the Upper School, and (at the end of the Long Walk) a tower which contains the Head Master's "Chambers" on the ground-floor and a large class-room above. Facing the wall, on the opposite side of the road, is a long line of boarding-houses, and at the farther end, in the angle where the road branches right and left, are the "New" Schools (as they have been stupidly denominated), that were erected in 1862-3 to accommodate the constantly increasing overflow from the odd corners in the old buildings, which were then the only class-rooms. In naming this new building—which is imposing enough in itself, though somewhat out of character with its neighbours—an excellent opportunity was lost of doing honour to the memory of Provost Hawtrey, that courteous gentleman and refined scholar, than whom Eton never had a worthier Head, and who closed a career devoted to her interests during the progress of the work to which we are alluding. There are thirteen class-rooms in the New Schools, and two large apartments, one of which has been used in relief of the Chapel. The internal arrangements are very superior to those which exist in the old rooms, all of which are situated in the School Yard, whither we will now proceed.

The School Yard is the larger of the two quadrangles of which the College originally consisted. It is about 75 yards long by 50 wide, and is completely shut in by buildings, with the exception of a short piece of dead wall in the S.E. corner. There are three approaches in use, of the usual collegiate character, *viz.* mere doorways in the surrounding buildings. The principal entrance is from the Long Walk, by "College Gates," under Upper School. It is quite plain, as may be observed in our etching. At this entrance the lofty Clock Tower, rising directly opposite, in the centre of the east side of the quadrangle, must of necessity be the first object that catches the eye. The clock, which gives its name to the edifice, albeit that it treats Greenwich authority with contempt, rules the time despotically at Eton; and woe to the boy whose watch ventures to disagree with its arbitrary assertions! Fortunately, its utterances are as a rule clear, if not correct; but when, as occasionally happens, the great automaton does that which a living workman apparently cannot do—gives up striking, a state of anarchy prevails, of which the more unwilling of the clock's subjects take full advantage.

THE CLOCK TOWER.

On either side of the Clock Tower are rooms belonging to the Lodge (the Provost's residence). In the tower itself is the spacious apartment called "Election Chamber," being the place where the Provost of King's College, Cambridge—to which, as Mr. Pote observes in his "Registrum Regale," Eton annually sends her ripe fruit—and his two "Posers"* meet the Eton authorities for the purpose of electing scholars of Eton to Scholarships at King's.

The Chapel occupies nearly the whole of the south side of the Yard, and the Lower School and the Collegers' quarters form the north side. Upper School and the Head Master's Room, with their respective staircases, complete the square. In the centre is a Statue placed there by Provost Godolphin, "perenni memoriæ pientissimi principis, Henrici Sexti, Regis Angliæ et Ffranciæ, et Domini Hiberniæ, Collegii Etonensis ffundatoris munificentissimi."

THE UPPER SCHOOL is not the original building that occupied its site. It was built at a cost of £1500, by Provost Allestree, an eminent Royalist, who died in 1680, and he employed no less distinguished an architect than Sir Christopher Wren. It is supported on the School Yard side upon a lofty colonnade of eleven arches, though on the outer side, as we have seen, there are ground-floor rooms beneath it. The entrance is at the top of a fine old oak staircase, which ascends from the south end of the colonnade, and is common to both the School and the Chapel, the floor of the latter being on an equally high level. Our artist's sketch of the old stairs will awaken recollections of many an unruly scrimmage in "Fourth Form" days, when some 150 boys were surging about on them, waiting for "all up" (as the commencement of school was suggestively termed), or were all endeavouring to be the first down them at the end of the imprisonment. On these occasions, hats and books more frequently preceded than accompanied their respective owners, but as it merely ended in a redistribution of property, and a well-creased hat and coverless book are (or at any rate *were*) in accordance with Fourth Form ideas of what is "jolly," no one seemed any the worse.

Upper School is a long room, ninety-five feet by thirty, capable of holding about 600 boys, when closely packed, as is demon-

---

* Examiners. The old word "pose" signifies heaviness.—*Johnson.*

strated on those days on which the Sixth Form have to make "Speeches" (recitations) before as many of their school-fellows as can be crammed in. The number of class-rooms being still insufficient, three or four Masters take their forms "in school" there

UPPER SCHOOL STAIRS.

at the same time. These "divisions" are separated from each other by heavy red curtains, as the Courts in Westminster Hall used to be before the excrescence on the west side of it was erected for their accommodation. There are five boxes, or "desks," from which the Masters preside over their respective divisions. Dr. Keate's division consisted of the first 200 boys in the school, and it was from the large desk at the upper end of the room that he daily went through the farce of pretending to instruct this unmanageable assembly, and it was in that same desk that he was screwed up by the boys while they were at " saying lesson," and then pelted, and over the sides of which he escaped, calling at the top of his voice, " I'll flog you all ! "

Upper School is the place where the half-yearly " Trials " —examinations for promotion—take place. Round the walls are the busts of eighteen Eminent Etonians—it would perhaps be invidious to say the eighteen *most* eminent, considering some of those who are comprised in the list of absentees. A simple name on each bust, without title or date, is amply sufficient to justify its *raison d'être.*   Here are the names :—

HOWE	PORSON	NORTH
GRAY	DENMAN	WELLINGTON
HAMMOND	GREY	GRENVILLE
CANNING	HALLAM	PEARSON
WELLESLEY	FIELDING	CHATHAM
FOX	WALPOLE	CAMDEN

Some of these names, and countless others, belonging to more humble individuals, are carved on the panels, desks, and seats in every direction.   The older ones were done—presumably "on the sly "—with no attempt at method, by the boys themselves; but for many years it has been the custom for every boy on leaving to have his name properly cut by a deputy; and as every square inch of wood in Upper School was used up ten years ago, the names since then have been methodically carved in regular order upon some new oak panels on the staircase leading down from the HEAD MASTER'S ROOM, which is at the north end of Upper School, and communicating with it, and better known as the " Swishing Room," from a performance that not unfrequently takes place there.   In this room the Head Master takes his division in school. It consists of the twenty Sixth-Form —ten of whom are invariably Collegers and ten Oppidans— and the first twelve of the Upper Fifth, and is denominated " Doctor's Division." On the walls of the room are several copies of ancient reliefs; and on a pedestal in a prominent position is a bust of Henry Pelham, fourth Duke of New-castle, K.G., who in 1829 founded the Scholarship which bears his name. This much-coveted prize is the principal distinction that Eton has to give; it is worth in money and books £50 a year for three years, and confers the blue riband of classical scholarship in the school for the time being. The second in merit receives a gold medal, and the next best up are termed " the Select."

The names of the Scholars and Medallists are inscribed on panels immediately behind the Duke's bust, and it appears that the chief distinction has been gained 25 times by Collegers, and on 20 occasions by Oppidans. Among those who have been NEWCASTLE SCHOLARS are the following :—the Hon. Sir Edward Creasy (1831), Chief Justice of Ceylon, Author of " Eminent Etonians ;" the late Vice-Chancellor Sir John Wickens (1833) ; C. J. Bayley, Esq. (1835), C.B., Governor of the Bahamas ; the Ven. Edward Balston (1836), Archdeacon of Derby, late Head Master of Eton ; and the Rev. Henry Hotham (1839), Vice-Master of Trin. Coll., Cambridge. Lord Lyttelton (1834) ; Canon Birch (1838), late tutor to the Prince of Wales ; Henry Hallam (1840), son of the Historian ; and Professor Goldwin Smith (1841) were Medallists. Nine of the Scholars and five Medallists (exclusive of those who afterwards gained the Scholarship) are, or have been, Assistant Masters in the School.

We have said that the Head Master's room is commonly called the " Swishing Room," and no visitor will fail to observe the " block" upon which the executions take place,—not but that the two steps of which it consists form a very harmless-looking piece of furniture. Flogging with a birch has from time immemorial been the regular constitutional punishment at Eton ;

it is administered by the Head Master only, and no other kind of corporal punishment is permitted; the corrective power of the Assistant Masters being limited to imposing tasks of extra work (too frequently of a useless, instead of an improving character), and to making offenders present themselves at unusual hours. If an Assistant wants to go beyond this, he must send the boy to the Head Master. The consequence is that there is necessarily much more flogging than at those schools where the assistant masters have the right of caning; and it is far better that it should be so, as the Eton system ensures deliberation and uniformity, in both of which the other is defective. There are many, no doubt, to whom the mere mention of this subject is like a red cloth to a bull, but we venture to assert that if corporal punishment is not an absolute necessity in a great public school, at any rate it is the mode of punishment least open to objection. If a boy has to write out lines, he is compelled to waste time which he might be spending profitably, besides ruining his handwriting and acquiring disgust for the subject-matter of his punishment; and, on the other hand, it is impossible to give him extra profitable work without unduly working the master, who, having imposed the task, is bound to see that it is correctly done. Again, shutting him up, or breaking up his play-time keeps him from healthy exercise, and is injurious to his physical development. But a moderate flogging has none of these disadvantages; it is found to be very deterrent, and yet interferes neither with a boy's work nor with his play. The only argument used against the system—*viz.*, that it degrades and brutalises those who are subjected to its operation—is so purely hypothetical and so completely refuted by hundreds of living instances, that to expend words upon it would be the most unprofitable supererogation. The extent to which flogging is resorted to, of course varies according to the views entertained on the subject by different Head Masters. It is related* of Dr. Barnard who was in that position, in the middle of last century,

---

* Hakewill's Hist. of Windsor.

that " he had that power of impressing his dictates and opinions on his scholars, which lessened the necessity of the detestable practice of corporeal correction." We expect that Dr. Barnard reduced " the necessity " from a rate which would be considered uncommonly high now-a-days, and the peculiar power of this model Head—an Eton Arnold—was not possessed by his successor Dr. Foster, who reigned from 1765 to 1773, and of whom we read that he was "a strict disciplinarian, severe against all immoral conduct, inexorable when he discovered meditated deception, and considering the deviation from truth to be an act of baseness which it would be equally wrong to pass without correction as to commit "; but " not being able to adopt his predecessor's mode of management and regulation, he rested upon and employed the severity of discipline." Doubtless he was the original of the tyrannical schoolmaster in the nursery rhyme :—

> " Dr. Foster is a good man ;
> He whips his pupils all he can.
> Out of England, into France,
> With his rod he makes them dance.
> From France he whips them into Spain,
> And thence he whips them back again."

Dr. Heath was called "Ascot" Heath, a name which speaks for itself; and Dr. Keate, as is well known, was another great *upholder* of the birch ; indeed his fame is chiefly associated with that portion of his duties. " Flog you, flog you," seems to have been his most constant utterance, and his one uniform sentence for every class of offence. Since his time writing out hundreds of lines—Georgics, Æneids, Books of Milton, &c.—has been substituted to a considerable extent for corporal punishment; but the block is by no means discarded. By the common-law of the School no Sixth Form boy is liable to be " swished," and by custom the same immunity is practically extended to the Upper and Middle Fifth.

Beyond the " Swishing Room " is a staircase leading down into the colonnade, at the bottom of which is the outer door of the Head Master's Chambers. In this apartment the assistant-masters assemble for a few minutes every day for the purpose of comparing notes among themselves and consulting their chief. As the Head Master takes no pupils a very moderate portion of his time is consumed in teaching, for the amount of work done "in school" is small compared with that done in "pupil-room." He has however a great deal of extremely heavy work in connection with the numerous examinations which take place, besides the general superintendence of the whole school and special charge of the Collegers.

The following is a list of THE HEAD MASTERS from 1756 to the present time:—

1756. Dr. EDWARD BARNARD.	1834. Dr. EDWARD CRAVEN HAWTREY.
1765. Dr. JOHN FOSTER.	
1773. Dr. JONATHAN DAVIES.	1853. Dr. CHARLES OLD GOODFORD.
1792. Dr. GEORGE HEATH.	
1802. Dr. JOSEPH GOODALL.	1862. Dr. EDWARD BALSTON.
1809. Dr. JOHN KEATE.	1868. Dr. JAMES JOHN HORNBY.

Since the creation of the Parliamentary Governing Body it is impossible that the Head Master can be the great man that he was. It is true that he formerly required the acquiescence of the Provost in his proceedings, but whether they agreed or not, they always managed to arrange matters quietly; and a formal written censure upon the Head Master such as the new Governing Body lately issued, and which found its way to the newspapers, was a thing quite inconceivable under the old régime. Whether the experiment of governing an institution like Eton by means of a committee of public men, collected in a most haphazard manner, and without any bond of union or necessary acquaintance with its subjects, will prove successful, is an anxious question which we must leave to the arbitrament of another generation. Like most other sweeping reforms, it would have been avoided but for the obstinate conservatism with which for many years reasonable and necessary changes were met by the powers that were.

The Head Master's residence—an edifice unpretentious to an extreme—is situated just at the back of his Chambers, on one side of a triangular plot called WESTON'S YARD. Here are also the Boys' Library, in which stands a bust of the late Prince Consort, who showed his interest in Eton, and at the same time his appreciation of one of her great deficiencies, by founding Prizes for Modern Languages; the New Buildings for Collegers, erected within the last thirty years; and THE PROVOST'S LODGE— or rather the entrance thereto; for that spacious residence, containing two complete suites of rooms, forms the north-west angle of the Cloister quadrangle, and is almost entirely shut out from view. Within are the pictures of several Provosts, in company with those of two ladies—Queen Elizabeth and Jane Shore. The connection of the latter with the College authorities is unascertained.

The appointment to the Provostship is nominally vested in the Fellows, but practically it is in the hands of the Crown, whose congé d'elire has in every instance been ultimately successful, though not without occasional attempts on the part of the Fellows to evade it on technical grounds.

Henry Sever was the first Provost, and there have been many distinguished men among his successors, of whom the first was William of Waynflete, successively Head Master of Winchester and Eton, Provost of Eton, Bishop of Winchester, and Lord High Chancellor. Among the others may be mentioned Sir Henry Savile, who founded the Savilian professorships of astronomy and geometry, at Oxford; Sir Henry Wotton, ambassador and statesman; and Francis Rowse, a distinguished Puritan writer and one of the Lords of Cromwell's Upper House, who died 1658 and was succeeded by an eminent Royalist, Dr. Allestree, who built the Upper School. Boyle, the Philosopher, who had been an Oppidan, was offered the Provostship, but declined it; and Waller, the Poet, also an Oppidan, was actually appointed to the post, but being a layman the Chancellor would have none of him. The list of later PROVOSTS is as follows:—

1791. Dr. JONATHAN DAVIES.   1853. Dr. EDWARD CRAVEN
1809. Dr. JOSEPH GOODALL.   HAWTREY.
1840. Rev. FRANCIS HODG-   1862. Dr. CHARLES OLD GOOD-
       SON, B.D.   FORD.

The buildings at the base of Weston's Yard are common to it and to the north side of the School Yard, the two spaces being

LOWER SCHOOL PASSAGE.

connected by "Lower School Passage," from whence the staircase ascends to "Long Chamber" and the other apartments for Collegers, which together constitute the upper floor of this side of the yard. In the passage itself the old panels are thickly inscribed up to the ceiling with the names of departed Collegers. On the

right, as you enter from Weston's Yard, are the doors of the old
Lower School, a murky region, but little known even among
Etonians, which has recently, under the new Bismarckian régime,
been annexed to the great Upper School; not, however, before
the majority of its diminutive inhabitants, needlessly alarmed at
the increase of their more powerful neighbours, had revolted from
their Alma Mater and their legitimate Head, and migrated under
the experienced lead of a deservedly popular subordinate chief,
whose treason having proved successful is of course no treason.
The seceders could not leave old associations far behind, and the
prosperous colony which they established in the immediate neighbourhood sends many of its offspring back to the old place.   The
Third Form, meanwhile, has been absorbed into the Upper School,
and the First and Second Forms are altogether suppressed, leading,
it will be observed, to an anomalous system of numeration.   The
Lower Master—the ancient " Ostiarius "—having been deposed
from his throne at the top of the Lower School, has been provided
with a berth as Head of the Fourth Form; and it is understood that,
unlike the old woman whose case we have called attention to, he has
been compensated for his loss of the Lower School fees.   The old
Third Form was divided into " Upper Greek," " Lower Greek,"
" Sense,"* and " Nonsense,"* and these four divisions and a fifth,
composed of the First and Second Forms, were all taken in school
by different masters in the long room to which we have just
conducted our readers, and were not even separated by the inter-
position of a curtain; so that a considerable Babel was thus realised.
Immediately above Lower School is Long Chamber, the
dormitory of the twenty-one junior Collegers, each of whom has
now a space to himself partitioned off from the rest.   Up to thirty
years ago Long Chamber was twice its present size, extending almost
the whole length of the School Yard, but (with the exception of
three small rooms) the Collegers had no other accommodation than

---

* From the boys' progress in Latin versification.   *Sense* verses are intended to
be translatable.   *Nonsense* verses are words strung together so as " to scan " without
any regard to their meaning.

this gallery, in which they were all herded together. There " they were locked up at eight o'clock at night (in winter at five) and saw nobody again until half-past seven next morning."* Those were the days when Long Chamber was a bye-word for bullying, and the Foundation Scholarships went begging; a state of things no doubt in accordance with the pecuniary interests of the Provost and Fellows, but brought about by gross violations of their statutory duties towards the boys. During the last thirty years, however, prodigious changes have been effected in College, the improvement commencing under Provost Hodgson. Long Chamber has been split up, and part of it turned into studies, while the beds in the other part have been separated by partitions; and forty-nine out of the seventy Collegers are now provided with single rooms in the New Buildings. Moreover the feeding is of a far more generous character than formerly; and, in short, the King's Scholars of the present day are every bit as well off for board and lodging as their school-fellows the Oppidans.

We must now return to the School Yard by way of Lower School Passage. Immediately opposite this entrance is a flight of stone steps leading up to a porch and door in the centre of the north side of the Chapel. Thither our artist desires us to accompany him, for this portion of the grand edifice is suitable for an etching at close quarters, and the subject could not fail to be recognised by an Etonian wherever the picture was presented to him. On the broad upper step of the basement flight of CHAPEL STEPS the Head Master stands when he "calls absence," *i.e.* calls over the "school list" for the purpose of compelling attendance and discovering those who are absent. This performance, which lasts fully fifteen minutes, is of very frequent occurrence, and must be one of "the Head's" most tedious duties. He calls the names of all the Collegers and the Sixth and Fifth Form Oppidans—more than half the whole School; and the Assistant-Master who is "in desk" that week simultaneously renders a like service in another

---

* Report of Public School Commissioners.

Chapel steps

part of the School Yard to the Lower Boys.*   On a half
holiday there is "absence" at three o'clock and (in summer
time) again at six o'clock, and on a holiday at 11.30 a.m. as well.
The Upper Boys while being "called" stand in a circle at a
respectful distance from the Head Master; the Lower Boys
on the other hand crowd and jostle round their crier like
excursionists at a booking-office. The omission of Absence which
occasionally happens—of course quite unexpectedly—is termed
"a call," which is almost as far-fetched an expression as
"present at absence." In the bays formed by the Chapel buttresses the game of "Fives"† originated, the earliest "Court"
being the one depicted in our etching. The peculiarity of Eton
"Fives," and that which makes it far more skilful than the modi-
fication of the game played elsewhere, consists in the "pepper-
box," which is the name given to the space between a buttress
that is built out at right angles from the left side of all Eton courts
and a step that changes the level of the inner and outer parts
of the court. Such an obstruction was unlikely to have been
invented, and would be inexplicable, did not one know that the
game was originally adapted to a particular spot where the
"pepper-box" already existed (being formed by the end of the
stone balustrade of Chapel Steps), and that all the "Fives'
Walls" since erected at Eton have been constructed in accordance with this chance model. Having paused thus long on the
steps, let us enter the sacred building without further delay.

THE CHAPEL.

Eton College Chapel, the first stone of which was laid by King
Henry VI. on July 3, 1641, is a very handsome Gothic structure,
which, probably on account of the propinquity of so magnificent a

---

* All below the Fifth Form are termed "Lower Boys." Those in the Fifth and
Sixth Forms are "Upper Boys." These divisions must not be confounded with
those into Upper and Lower School which existed until very recently.

† Hand-rackets.

chapel as St. George's at Windsor, scarcely obtains its fair place
in public estimation.   It is 80 feet in height, 40 feet wide, and 175
feet long, including the Ante-chapel, which is 62 feet. In the length
there are eight bays on either side, formed by massive buttresses,
each containing a window 30 feet in height and 12 in width, with five
lights. The interior has none of that ornamental architecture which
does so much to adorn its more splendid sister at King's College,
Cambridge, and up to thirty years ago it was disfigured with a
hideous wainscot from the floor to the windows, and did not pos-
sess a pane of coloured glass.   Since that time the indifference of
the past has been retrieved with marvellous rapidity, and Eton
has now a place of worship in every respect worthy of her.   The
improvements commenced in 1842.   The whole of the wainscot-
ting, the unsightly pews, and a frightful organ loft which filled
up part of the Ante-chapel and the first bay of the Chapel were
removed;   and a beautifully carved oak screen was placed
between the choir and the Ante-chapel. Since then seventy Stalls,
elaborately carved, with spiral canopies, have been erected, every
window in the building has been filled with richly coloured glass,
and the east end has been gorgeously—perhaps too gorgeously
—decorated.   The College is indebted to the munificence of the
Rev. John Wilder, one of the present Fellows, for the stained glass
of no less than fourteen out of the sixteen large side windows. The
other two side windows were presented in 1849 by the Assistant
Masters and the Rev. W. A. Carter respectively, at the same time
that the grand East Window was put up by a subscription among
Old Etonians, and the window above the arch at the west end of
the choir by the Rev. Edward Coleridge. The Stalls were erected
between 1848 and 1854; many of them were presented by individuals, others by various combinations of Eton men, and the
remainder were obtained by a general fund raised among Etonians
for the purpose.   They are nearly all dedicated to eminent Etonians, a brass with a suitable inscription being in each case affixed
to the back of the stall. Among the distinguished men whose
connection with Eton is thus commemorated are—the "ever-

memorable" John Hales (1656); Oughtred, the mathematician (1660); Hammond, the divine (1662); Boyle, the philosopher (1691); Gray, the poet; Lord North; Lord Grenville; the Duke of Wellington—in whose stall the brass relates that some Etonians placed it there "invicto Europæ vindici pacis restitutori"; the Marquess Wellesley—"memoriæ viri in literarum cultu et in rerum administratione pariter felicis inter Etonenses suos juxta sepulti"; the Duke of Newcastle—his stall being erected by the Newcastle Scholars; Winthrop Mackworth Praed; Sir George Cathcart; Archbishop Summer; Bishops Pearson* (Chester), Bethell (Bangor), Sumner (Winchester), Gray (Capetown), Denison (Salisbury), Selwyn (Lichfield), and Chapman (Colombo); Provosts Waynflete ("strenuus felixque defensor†"), Westbury, Savile, Godolphin, Barnard, Davies, Goodall, Hodgson, and Hawtrey; and Dr. Keate. One stall was erected by the Cust family, who have never been without a representative in the school since Sir Purey Cust in 1654, and whose list includes Sir John Cust, Speaker from 1761 to 1770. Henry VI., Queen Victoria, the Prince Consort, and Queen Adelaide are commemorated with stalls as royal benefactors; but nobody seems to have remembered George III. in this distribution of seats. Stalls are however very properly assigned to the memory both of the Rev. Charles Luxmoore, late Fellow, who was foremost in promoting the grand work of which they form parts; and of Jacob Rattee, of Cambridge, who designed it and carried it out.

In the Ante-chapel there are five large windows, all of which are now filled with painted glass. The central window at the west end was erected by some old Etonians in 1851, and beneath it stands a fine statue of the Founder by Bacon, which was placed there in 1786 at a cost of £600 bequeathed for the purpose by Rev. E. Betham, a Fellow. The window on the north side of it is a memorial to Mr. T. G. Farquhar, who fell at the battle of Aliwal in 1846, aged 19; and the third of the west-end triplet was the last in the whole chapel

---

* Writer " on the Creed." † See page 2.

to remain in its original state, the coloured glass being the gift of Dr. Balston while he was Head Master. The two beautiful windows in the north and south walls of the Ante-chapel constitute the " Crimean Memorial," erected by subscription in 1859 in memory of the Etonians who fell during the Russian War. The arms and names of these devoted and deeply-lamented soldiers are inscribed upon shields and scrolls painted on the walls beneath the windows ; and we venture to think there are few things so touching as the perusal in a School Chapel of a memorial list of its alumni whose lives have been sacrificed in maintaining the honour of their country before the enemy, especially when it is clear that many of those named must have gone almost straight from the mimic battles of school to their premature but ever-glorious deaths.

The following is a list of the Etonians who are thus commemorated. Their names are placed on the Chapel walls in no sort of order; but we prefer to group them chronologically in the order in which they fell, premising that any mistakes in the names must be attributed to the ill-formed old English characters used—in accordance with a provoking conventionality—in the original list.

Name.	*Cause and date of death.*
Capt. G. Duckworth, 5th Dr. Gds. - - -	Illness at Varna, Aug. 24th, 1854.
„ C. G. Sutton, 23rd Fusiliers - - -	Illness in the Crimea, Sept. 15th ,,
Major E. Wellesley, Asst. Quar.-Master Gen. -	,, ,, ,, 20th ,,
Capt. H. W. Cust, Coldstream Gds. - -	Killed at the Alma, ,, ,, ,,
„ F. E. Evans, 23rd Fusiliers - - -	,, ,, ,, ,, ,,
Lieut. F. Luxmoore, 30th Regt. - - -	,, ,, ,, ,, ,,
Capt. Hon. C. L. Hare, 7th Fusiliers - -	Wounds at ,, ,, 22nd ,,
„ E. H. L. Crofton, 77th Regt. - -	Illness - ,, 26th ,,
Lieut.-Col. A. Cox, Gren. Gds. - - -	,, - ,, 27th ,,
Capt. J. A. Freeman, Scots Greys - - -	,, - ,, 29th ,,
Lieut. J. Molesworth, 7th Fusiliers - -	,, - Oct. 5th ,,
Col. Hon. F. G. Hood, Gren. Gds. - -	Killed in the trenches, ,, 18th ,,
Lieut. H. A. Sparke, 4th Dragoons - -	,, in Balaklava Charge, Oct. 25, ,,
Lieut.-Gen. Hon. Sir G. Cathcart, G.C.B., 4th Div.	,, at Inkerman, Nov. 5th, ,,
Lieut.-Col. J. H. Blair, M.P., Fusilier Gds. -	,, ,, ,, ,, ,,
„ J. C. M. Cowell, Coldstream Gds. -	,, ,, ,, ,, ,,
„ C. F. Seymour, Fusilier Gds. - -	,, ,, ,, ,, ,,
Major H. G. Wynne, 68th Regt. - - -	,, ,, ,, ,, ,,
„ J. B. Sharpe, 20th Regt. - - -	,, ,, ,, ,, ,,
Capt. F. H. Ramsden, Coldstream Gds. - -	,, ,, ,, ,, ,,
„ Hon. H. A. Neville, Gren. Gds. - -	,, ,, ,, ,, ,,

Name.	*Cause and date of death.*
Capt. H. M. Bouverie (*a*), Coldstream Gds. - -	Killed at Inkerman, Nov. 5th, 1854.
,, Hon. G. C. C. Eliot, Coldstream Gds. -	,, ,, ,, ,, ,,
Lieut. L. N. Malcolm, Rifle Brigade - -	,, ,, ,, ,, ,,
,, H. Thorold, 33rd Regt. - - -	,, ,, ,, ,, ,,
,, F. B. Davies, Gren. Gds. - - -	Wounds bef. Sebastopol, Nov. 10th ,,
Cornet Hon. G. Neville, 5th Dr. Gds. - -	,, in bat. of Balaklava ,, 11th ,,
Lieut. J. H. U. Spalding, R.N., H.M.S. "London"	Killed in the trenches, Jan. 21st, 1855.
,, L. Kekewich, 20th Regt. - - -	Wounds Feb. 16th ,,
,, H. W. Wilberforce, R.N., H.M.S. "Hawke"	Over-exertion in Baltic ,, 20th ,,
Capt. R. H. P. Crawford, 90th Regt. - -	Illness - - ,, 24th ,,
Major A. F. Platt, 49th Regt. - - -	,, - - Mar. 10th ,,
Rev. C. H. Proctor, Asst. Chaplain 3rd Division -	,, - - ,, ,, ,,
Capt. A. Lempriere, 77th Regt. - - -	Attacking Rifle Pits Apr. 19th ,,
Lieut. S. A. Y. Benyon, 63rd Regt. - - -	From exposure May 22nd ,,
Col. L. W. G. Yea, 7th Fusiliers, com. stormg. party	Killed in attack on Redan, June 18th ,,
Capt. E. R. Forman, Rifle Brigade - -	,, ,, ,, ,, ,, ,,
Lieut. O. G. S. Davies, 38th Regt. - - -	,, ,, ,, ,, ,, ,,
,, F. R. Hurt, 34th Regt. - - -	,, ,, ,, ,, ,, ,,
Capt. Hon. J. W. Hely-Hutchinson, 13th Dragoons	Illness - - July 2nd ,,
Lieut. C. A. P. Boileau (*b*), Rifle Brigade - -	Wounds at attack on Redan, Aug. 1st ,,
Capt. D. F. B. Buckley, Scots Fusilier Gds. -	Killed in the trenches Sept. 7th ,,
,, H. M. Vaughan, 90th Regt. - - -	Wounds on Sept. 8, at Redan ,, 13th ,,
,, J. B. Marshall, 4th Dragoons - - -	Illness - - ,, 20th ,,
,, H. Townsend, 14th Regt. - - -	,, - - Nov. 29th ,,
Major H. L. Thompson, C.B., E.I.C. Service -	Over-exertion at Kars, June 13th, 1856.
Capt. W. W. Maitland, 49th Regt. - -	,, in Crimea, Nov. 15th ,,

Erroneously spelt in memorial thus—(*a*) Bouveire, (*b*) Boileam.

The Provost of Eton College has hitherto been ex-officio Rector of the parish of Eton, but under the new parliamentary régime this will not be the case in future. Originally the parish was possessed of a church, but on its falling into disrepair years ago, the inhabitants were permitted to use the College Chapel, and did so until the increase of the School rendered it impossible to continue this makeshift. In 1851 a new church was erected in High Street, as a chapel of ease, to which the parishioners removed; but it was not long before the College Chapel again overflowed. The whole School was just able to find room till 1857, when the Lower School was squeezed out and migrated to the Cemetery Chapel, and a few years later the Fourth Form also "swarmed," and settled upon one of the large rooms in the New Schools, whence they afterwards removed to a spacious chamber beyond Keate's Lane, where service has since been conducted at the same hours as at the Chapel. Until within the last few

                    The Choir.

years Eton College, its statutes notwithstanding, had no choir of
its own, but was content to hire the St. George's Choir on certain
afternoons and to go without any on other occasions. This system,
besides being cheap, had at any rate the advantage of variety,
and possibly was intended to impress upon the boys that their
pastors had no leaning towards any particular ritual; and moreover on those occasions when the Provost and Fellows *did* provide
a choir they were entitled to say that it was the best that could be
got in the country. However the Commissioners of 1864 had
new-fangled notions about statutory obligations, and made some
strong "recommendations" on the subject; whereupon (whether
post hoc or propter hoc we cannot say) the connexion with the
St. George's Choir was terminated, and the first attempts of Eton
College to get on without it were of the most painful description;
but after a while a real effort was made, and the Eton College
Choir can now not only "run alone," but what is more important
sing together. So warmly indeed has the musical element in the
Chapel services been taken up, that for a slight gain in that
respect the beauty of the building has been to a great extent
sacrificed by the re-erection in a modified form of the organ-loft
between the Chapel and the Ante-chapel, the removal of which
was one of the greatest of the improvements which were effected
thirty years ago.

The vaults beneath the Chapel are very capacious : in them are
deposited the remains of several Provosts, of John Longland,
Bishop of Lincoln, confessor to Henry VIII., of Richard Lord
Grey of Wilton, henchman to the same monarch, and of the
Marquess Wellesley. The last interment was that of Provost
Hawtrey, which took place in 1862 in the presence of the whole
school. On the walls of the Ante-chapel there are a great
number of monumental brasses to the memory of those buried
beneath, and of others connected with the place who lie else-
where. The most recent are respectively in memory of Vice
Chancellor Sir L. Shadwell, Mr. Justice Patteson, Dr. Keate, Dr.
Hawtrey, and Rev. H. Dupuis, Vicar of Richmond. The most

Chapel from the Clump

remarkable epitaph is that over the grave of Sir H. Wotton, Provost, who appears to have indulged in the use of strong metaphor—

> " Hic jacet sententiæ primus auctor—
> Disputandi pruritus sit ecclesiarum scabies—
> Nomen alias quære."

With that we will take our leave of the Chapel, our view of which is sketched from under Brocas Clump, a spot about half a mile off, to which we will presently introduce those who care to continue longer in our company.

THE CLOISTERS.

Leaving the Chapel by the steps into the School Yard, a few paces brings us to THE CLOISTERS, of which the entrance is under the Clock Tower. Of the row of buildings common to both Cloisters and School Yard one half, exclusive of the Tower, is taken up, on the first floor, by a most capacious apartment called " Election Hall," the reception room of the Provost's Lodge, to which also belongs greater part of the north side of the Cloisters. Over the south side is the College Library, containing a large and (it is said) most valuable collection of books : these literary coverts are, however, very strictly preserved by the College, and there are few who know anything of them ; indeed there is a notion that the game is not often disturbed even by the owners, though it would certainly be strange if the new amateur Fellows should have looked into everything except these books, even allowing for their preference for turning over new leaves.

The COLLEGE HALL is entered from and is parallel to this side of the Cloisters ; and its floor, like that of the Chapel, is several feet above the level of the ground. Though somewhat disproportioned to the large scale on which the other College buildings were constructed, it is sufficiently spacious, and its roof being laid bare to the top gives to the interior a very lofty appearance.

It was thoroughly restored about 20 years ago at the expense of the Rev. J. Wilder, the munificent Fellow who has done so much

                              The Hall.

for the College. On this occasion the original fire-places were discovered and opened out. There is one on either side and a third at the upper end ; each being of a size sufficient to roast an ox, though perhaps unsuited for the purpose, as the animal could escape by the chimney.

On the walls are several pictures of distinguished men who were formerly Collegers, including Sir Robert Walpole, Lord

THE COLLEGE PUMP.

Chancellor Camden, Sir Vicary Gibbs, Archbishop Sumner, Bishop Lonsdale, Lord Stratford de Redcliffe, the diplomatist of the Crimean War, and Sir J. Patteson and Sir J. T. Coleridge, Justices of the Queen's Bench, who were brothers-in-law in more senses than one.

At the foot of the Hall stairs, stands the old College Pump, which brings up from a great depth an unlimited supply of the coldest and purest water.   In summer-time the Pump is frequently resorted to by "wet-bobs"—from members of "the Eight" down to "bows" in "House Sweepstakes"—for the purpose of submitting their brachial muscles to the strengthening properties of an icy flow.   As to its beverage, it is so "curiously fine" that the Temperance Leaguers will no doubt buy the whole place up, if ever they persuade themselves to act up to their principles.

The remaining portion of the Cloisters are occupied by the Fellows of the old Foundation, and it is impossible to pass their doors and see their names on the trim brass plates without a pang of regret, that this dignified race of old gentlemen, who by their courtesy, benevolence and general high bearing, cannot but have exercised an influence for good in the place, is now moribund, and doomed to die out; to which may be added the mortifying reflection, that but for the want of a little political wisdom they might have been saved.   At the N.E. corner of the quadrangle is a narrow aperture leading to the Playing Fields, of which we will take advantage, in order to escape from a too prolonged sojourn amidst brick and mortar into the scenes of natural beauty which lie beyond.

III.

THE PLAYING FIELDS.

PREMISING the possibility that our taste is warped by an excessive sentiment in favour of our Alma Mater, we beg to record our unfaltering conviction that there is not on earth a place so delightful as the Eton " Playing Fields." The spot so called is, in truth, a perfect little " park," with water, timber, and green-sward charmingly blended. The silvery Thames, as yet triumphant over his enemies the Sewers, glides rapidly along the front, while the enclosed space is bisected by a humble but friendly tributary during the last reach of its independent existence. The trees are for the most part elms of the largest size, many of which, we grieve to say, having existed beyond the usual 300 years of elm-life, are no longer able to withstand the attacks of wintry gales, and are becoming more and more dismembered in each succeeding year. The grass throughout is sheep-fed, and large plots dedicated to cricket are kept as trim and even as lawns. Our artist has favoured us with three views of this locality. The first taken from the river (p. 8) we have already had reason to allude to. The " Sixth Form Bench " will be observed in the deep shade on the right, but why the seat should be so named we cannot explain. A considerable experience enables us to state that the Sixth Form never sit there, though members of the Third Form occasionally use it when engaged in the repair of minnow nets. The next view is that of " Sheep's Bridge," which is in the centre of the park, and at the spot where the trees are thickest. It spans the before-mentioned stream, which takes its name, we may add, from Chalvey, its native village. To the right of the little bridge and parallel to " Chalvey " is an artificial piece of

Sheep's Bridge
R.S.C. 187

water called " Fellows' Pond," which the pre-reformation Fellows doubtless kept well supplied with fish for Fridays; and the path on the narrow strip of ground between the pond and the brook, and on past Sheep's Bridge to Sixth Form Bench, bears the name of " Poet's Walk " in honour of Gray. Under the trees here in summer-time the members of " Upper Club "—*i.e.* the cricketers of the greatest prowess—enjoy the privilege of having an al-fresco tea. The term " Upper Club " is applied however not only to the society of players, but also to the ground on which they play. Similarly there is " Middle Club " and " Lower Club," and moreover there is a bit of ground known as " Aquatics " from the fact that it is the piece allotted to those who are in " the Boats," and whose cricket is presumably too gross to be tolerated in one of the regular games. Upper Club is the subject of our third view in the Playing Fields. It is the place where " the Eleven " play the " school matches," and is probably the most beautiful cricket ground in the country, having a dense background of magnificent trees. At the same time it must be admitted that from a high cricketing point of view it is not a desirable pitch for a wicket, as it is *too* true and not sufficiently " lively;" and there can be no doubt that the extreme dissimilarity between this ground and " Lord's " has been a signal disadvantage to Eton in the public school matches. For all that, Etonians would on no account exchange their " Upper Club," as will be readily understood by any one who has visited the spot during the progress of a match on a fine afternoon in June.

Eton is divided into " wet-bobs " and " dry-bobs "—aquatics and cricketers—the proportions being about equal, and the Playing Fields are to the latter what the River is to the former. Here the Captain of the Eleven and there the Captain of the Boats respectively exercise a sway as despotic and irresponsible as that of the Shah himself, though fortunately a very great deal more beneficial to those who are subjected to it. In winter-time, however, the distinction between " wet-bob " and " dry-bob " is to a great extent in abeyance, as Football is t' en the pastime common

to both.   But the exigencies of cricket grounds are such that very
little football is permitted in the Playing Fields, and none whatever on Upper Club.   There is a species of football, however,
peculiar to Eton, called the "Wall Game," which is not only
carried on in the Playing Fields, but could scarcely be played
anywhere else, as it is a purely local game adapted to the long
piece of wall which bounds part of the Playing Fields from the
Slough Road.   As only twenty-two can use "the wall" at the same
time, the game is limited to the élite of the school, and many a
boy passes through Eton without any experience of it as a player.
To describe the game on paper to any one who had not studied it
on the spot would occupy more than our whole space, and we
must therefore be excused from attempting it.   Those who desire
to see it, should visit Eton on the morning of St. Andrew's day,
when according to immemorial custom a match is annually played
" at the wall " between the Collegers and Oppidans.   It is however but a stupid game for spectators, though an extremely
attractive one for players, and especially for those lovers of
football who, being in physique like Hamlet, are unable to move
with rapidity in the "field game."   Formerly the "Playing
Fields " were known as the " Shooting Fields," a designation the
park obtained either from the sporting proclivities of the Fellows
with regard to the young rooks in the Easter holidays, or from the
fact that the boys received instruction there in archery at a time
when proficiency therein led to results more important than prizes
at the meetings of Toxopholite Societies.

IV.

THE RIVER.

OUR artist is now keen for river scenery, and requires our company for an aquatic expedition. Just below the Playing Fields the South Western Railway takes advantage of an island to cross the river, and close to the bridge is a picturesque fishing cottage,

BLACK POTS.

rejoicing in the uneuphonious name of " Black Pots." It belongs to the present Head Master of Eton, and is the place where in 1869 the " Oxford Four," of whom three were Old Etonians, trained for the great international boat race against the American University of Harvard. We can go no further *down* stream than this point, for our labours are strictly

Etonian, and the river below Windsor is forbidden to the boys, except as a practising course to " the Eight " when preparing for Henley. From Black Pots Windsor Bridge may be reached either by returning through the Playing Fields and College, or less circuitously by crossing the river and pursuing the right bank.   In the latter case we shall pass Windsor Lock, or " Romney Pound "—as it is locally called—with its pretty peep of the Castle on one side, and its full view of the College on the other,

THE RAFTS.

both of which are duly depicted in this series ; and further on the Weir, and the " Masters' Bathing Place " thereat; and then we shall find ourselves on the narrow breakwater called " the Cobler," * whence we shall require a boat in order to attain the rafts on the other side of Windsor Bridge.

If you would view these Rafts aright, you should *not* go there

---

* The derivation is Cobbe-laire, " Swan's Nest."

by moonlight, because Eton boys are " locked up " about the time the sun sets, and what you ought to see is the extraordinary rush that takes place on to the rafts a few minutes after " an absence has been called." Pelting " down town " come those energetic " wet-bobs," who are determined to see Maidenhead, or at least Monkey Island, before they are " wanted " again at College, and in less than ten minutes since they answered to their names in the School-yard, they have changed all their clothes, pushed off their boats, and are pulling away at a pace apparently intended for

ST. GEORGE'S CHAPEL AND CURFEW TOWER, WINDSOR CASTLE.

a hundred yards' burst, but in truth to be maintained for many a mile. A few minutes more and the rafts swarm with less active votaries of the oar, for whom a paddle up to " Athens " and a bathe will suffice for the afternoon's pastime. Over the boat-houses in our sketch are numerous upper chambers in which the high hats, black coats and white ties of Eton scholastic life are doffed and replaced by flannel garments of every variety of check and colour. Just beyond the boat-houses is " the Brocas " (or " Brockhurst "), the publicus ager of Eton, an extensive meadow on the river bank, which is well known to many as the place where the numerous visitors to Eton on the " Fourth of June " assemble to witness the procession of Boats.   Here is obtained that grand view of the Castle and town of Windsor, with which Turner and many another artist have made the world familiar, and of which English-men may well be proud.   The Castle's greatest length is here seen—from the N.E. angle of the State Apartments on the left to the old Curfew Tower at the western extremity on the right; while the somewhat mean appearance of the town, crouching low at its foot, serves to bring out the grandeur of the royal residence in more striking relief.   Unfortunately in the portion nearest to the river, of which we give a sketch, including St. George's Chapel, the Horse Shoe Cloisters and the Curfew Tower, renova-tions of a most painful character have recently been carried out. The Curfew Tower itself, the oldest portion of the entire pile, is spoilt by a roof equally out of keeping with its date, character, and shape ; and the whole of this corner now presents an incon-gruous appearance, amounting to an eyesore, from the restoration of buildings which must always have been out of keeping with the main structure, the result of which is that red-brick houses with Elizabethan ornamental woodwork, high chimneys, tiled roofs and protruding attic windows, appear in provoking dissonance over the tops of grey battlements and embrasures in solid masonry. The island in our picture is known in Eton geography as " *the* Eyot " *par excellence*; it is the place from whence the display of fireworks takes place at the termination of the 4th of June regatta; but it will not be used for this or any other purpose much longer, unless, with the aid of its new camp-sheeting, it manages to resist further encroachments on the part of the stream.   The rail in the foreground will recall to an old " wet-bob " the day when with diffidence he first hired a "chance boat" and put forth into the deep.

When the back is turned on Windsor, "Brocas Clump," with its two dozen grand old elms massed together, becomes a striking

object; and then looking away from the river the eye is instantly attracted by Eton Chapel, which is the only College building lofty enough to be discernible from this point over the thick foliage in which the rest are enveloped. Formerly the view all round from the Brocas was extremely picturesque, especially of St. Leonard's Hill across the river; but it is now entirely spoilt by the Great Western Railway, which, in order to keep out of the floods that visit the Thames valley in winter, comes into Windsor for two miles upon arches. He must be a Philistine indeed who can look with patience on this hideous screen of brick and mortar : nevertheless as far as the " Great Western " is concerned it is doubtless a necessity, and as regards the Eton authorities it is a just retribution for their constant opposition to all the former schemes of the Railway Company. When the main line of the Great Western was planned, though railways had then been in existence ten years, Eton College, like Oxford University and other good old Tories, was horrified at the idea of so revolutionary a change in the conditions of locomotion, and joined with the Crown tooth and nail in driving the main line away from Windsor, through which place it would have been taken but for these adverse influences. They were not even satisfied with the proposal that the line should come no nearer than Slough, and Serjeant Mere-wether, in opposing the bill of 1835 before the Committee of the Lords, used language of which the following is a specimen. He said that if the railway were made " the Thames would be choked up for want of traffic, the drainage of the country destroyed, and Windsor Castle left unsupplied with water. As for Eton College it would be absolutely and entirely ruined : London would pour forth the most abandoned of its inhabitants to come down by the railway and pollute the minds of the scholars, whilst the boys themselves would take advantage of the short interval of their play-hours to run up to town, mix in all the dissipation of London life, and return before their absence could be discovered." * The

---

* " Life of Brunel," p. 73.

Commons had passed the bill in 1834, after a struggle for 52 days in Committee, but it was more than the Lords could swallow. In 1835 however the bill went through both Houses, five clauses having been inserted at the instance of Eton College providing that no station should be made near Eton and that persons should be specially employed to keep the boys off the railway. The Act having passed, the main line was made, and then naturally came the question in what way Windsor was to be connected with it. The Railway Company desired to skirt Eton College closely on the west side, to make a station near the present Mathematical School, and running at the back of High Street to cross the river at Brocas Rails. The College authorities however would have none of it, and that they were at least disinterested in their opposition may be inferred from the fact that they rejected an offer on the part of the Company to add a large piece of ground to the Playing Fields if permitted to carry out their scheme. The railway then took its present course, and the eyesore to which we have alluded is the result. The bridge which carries the line over the Thames will be observed in our etching just beyond Brocas Clump. It is one of Brunel's works, and was considerately made to cross the river at one span so as not to interfere with the boys' boating. It is a large example of the bow-and-string girder, the span being 202 feet and the height of the truss 23 feet. The works commenced in 1848 and the bridge was opened on October 8, 1849. An absurd notion is from time to time set on foot that this bridge is unsafe. We would, if it were of any use, give some account of the overwhelming tests to which it was subjected, but happily most people are content to believe that Brunel understood his business, and those who do not would not believe anything.

Just above the railway bridge as we ascend the river, a narrow back-water known as "Cuckoo Weir" rejoins the main stream, having separated from it about three-quarters of a mile higher up. In "Cuckoo Weir" are the bathing places for Third and Fourth Form Boys, which go by the names of "Italy" and

" Acropolis ; " the former is for those who are unable to swim, while the latter being a lofty mound for the purpose of taking "running headers" into deep water can only be used by those who have "passed" in swimming or are, at any rate, nearly competent to do so. The "Remove" bathe at "Upper Hope," and the Fifth Form at "Athens," both on the main stream, while the Sixth Form, "the Eight," and "the Eleven," and a few other "swells," have the privilege of bathing in the glorious rush of water under Boveney Weir. At all these bathing places the banks are supported by camp-sheeting, and the grass near the edge is kept like a lawn. At "Athens" part of the bank is raised so as to give a level run of some fifteen yards to the water, with a fall at the end of ten or twelve feet. This is the principal place for practising the "headers," for which Etonians are justly celebrated, the excellence of which consists in the distance cleared by the spring through the air and the instantaneous re-appearance of the head above water after its immersion. Here the Aquatic Games annually take place, when medals are awarded for swimming, diving, and "headers," and the winners are respectively dubbed the "Tachynectic," "Colymbetic," and "Cybestetic" "Professors;" and here also the swimming examination, or "Passing," as it is called, is held on frequent occasions during the summer school-time. Since the excellent rule was made and enforced, about thirty years ago, that no boy may go out in a boat until he has "passed" in swimming, there has been no case of drowning in the school, whereas before that time scarcely a year elapsed without a fatal catastrophe on the river. The motive for learning to swim is now so strong that the proportion of boys who go through Eton without doing so is insignificantly small; and besides its beneficial results on the spot, the new system has doubtless saved the life of many an Eton man after the conclusion of his school career.

Our view of BOVENEY LOCK and Weir-stream is taken from "Rushes," a well-known spot to all Eton oarsmen as the turning point in the course of the principal boat races, and the starting place in others. An Eton " wet-bob " is so much in the habit of getting over long distances in a short time that it never occurs to him that his race-course is considerably longer than that adopted anywhere else, the metropolitan champion course excepted. But so it is. The Rushes are a mile and three-quarters from Windsor Bridge; and " round Rushes " is the least distance that is thought anything of for a row, and (minus the first quarter of a mile going up) is the regular course for pair-oared and sculling races; though as longer boats would have a difficulty in turning a wrypeck while racing, the course for " eights " and " fours " is only *down* from " Rushes." The river between Windsor and Boveney, according to ordinary notions on the subject, is extremely

RUSHES.

ill-adapted for boat-racing, having no straight " reaches " of any length, but on the other hand a number of formidable bends, of which two—known as Upper and Lower Hope—are sharper than right angles. These inconveniences, however, tend to promote good watermanship, and have probably had some share in bringing about the marked success of Eton oarsmen, a success with which of late years the esteemed name of Warre has been intimately associated, and which culminated in 1867, when (with a solitary exception) every Henley Medal was carried off by an Etonian. We have said that the course " round Rushes " is of unusual length, but after all it is a trifle compared with the old Eton course. Before Boveney Lock was constructed—which is

Boveney Lock
R.S.C. 1873

not so very long ago—the course extended to the villa above Surly ; and the races, which in these days go round Rushes, then went on as far again before they turned, so that the rowers, when they got back to Windsor Bridge, could have had very little change out of seven miles. At the spot whence our view of Boveney is taken the immediate neighbourhood is flat and un-interesting, but the eye has only to be raised to be charmed, for Windsor Castle stands up grandly at the end of the reach, and on the one hand is St. Leonard's Hill, and on the other the lofty trees which conceal Eton College. In the latter direction is the " Sanatorium," a spacious red-brick building about half a mile from College, which happily is very rarely called into requisition, for though theorists have frequently demonstrated to their own satisfaction that Eton must be an unhealthy place, practical experience has proved the reverse ; and upon this hear, ye anxious parents, what the learned Collier wrote at the beginning of last century—" Eton is so called from its low situation among the waters ; for Eton is the same as Water-town, but as they are running waters and it is a gravelly soil, it is observed that no place is more healthy than this." That point settled, we turn again to Boveney ; and with a passing shudder at the frightful house which defaces the right bank below the Weir, and which the College bought to prevent its being opened as a " public," we pass on to the Lock, where we shall observe that boats are put through with a rapidity that all the old slow-coaches from the other Thames' Locks could not attain to if set to work together.

On a half-holiday " after four " this lock may be seen densely packed with eights, fours, pairs, and sculling boats so close that scarcely a square inch of the water that floats them is visible, and such is the alertness both of the lock-keeper and his young cus-tomers that in less than five minutes they are all out on the other side and speeding away in a gradually lengthening line. The Eton system of distributing " schools." and " absences " evenly throughout the day, so as to break it up into a number of short periods, and of giving the boys frequent rather than long intervals to themselves, is admirable for promoting habits of energy and alacrity, and for effecting the compression of a great deal of activity into a short space of time. In these respects the average "Eton Boy" of seventeen or eighteen contrasts favourably with the "University Man" of the ordinary stamp a year or two older. The latter, being comparatively independent of hours, saunters down to the river, the stable, or the cricket field, as the case may be, wastes an enormous amount of time in preliminaries, and spends a whole afternoon in one pursuit. The school-boy, on the other hand, having his half-holiday split up into three or four different periods, is obliged to be uncommonly quick in his movements in order to get through a game or to attain any distance worth speaking of; and having done it, and re-appeared, he is all ready for a fresh start at some other occupation. We can hardly expect our young friends still at school to concur in praising a regulation which naturally appears to them an irksome restraint, but we do not doubt that their future retrospect of its results will coincide with our own. It is unfortunately very true—unless indeed the new Governing Body have wrought wonders—that too little time, or rather too little attention, is given at Eton to the real work of school; but the supporters of Eton institutions may at least claim this merit for the place, that no such thing as sloth exists there, while the display of energy—misdirected though much of it be—is most striking. The boy who has "sapped" during time at his own disposal may not perhaps get from his companions the credit he deserves, but one who has "done nothing" is an object of universal contempt. It is surprising what distances the boys get in the time allowed them, $2\frac{3}{4}$ hours being considered sufficient for a row to Maidenhead and back (fourteen miles), including the run from College to the rafts, changing and re-changing clothes, and the return to College; and $2\frac{1}{4}$ hours being the full time occupied by "a run with the Beagles," from the boys' leaving school at 11.45 until their re-appearance clean and neat at dinner at two, during which interval they have "changed," gone upwards of a mile to "the kennels," and probably had a couple of "runs" over several miles of ploughed fields.

Though as a rule three hours is the extreme period which the boys can get to themselves without a break, there is an exception allowed with regard to half-holiday afternoons in summer time, on which occasions the cricketers playing in "Upper Club" game, and two crews of "the Boats" under parole not to row less than ten miles up the river before turning, are excused six o'clock absence, and thus obtain five and a half hours straight away. The cricketers have long enjoyed this privilege (called "Cricket Bill," from the list on which the names are sent in to the Head Master), but it was obtained by the Boats only twelve years ago, and in a way characteristic of the manner in which the authorities of our great public schools deal with the boys. There had been from "time immemorial" a custom for the "Upper Boats" on three different evenings in the Summer Half, called "Check Nights," to row up to Surly in their Regatta "checks" and there partake of a convivial supper, rowing down again afterwards in the best way they could. The authorities at length, with great reason, determined to abolish "Check Nights;" but instead of outraging the feelings of the whole school by an arbitrary edict, they "treated" with the Captain of the Boats on the subject, and it was solemnly determined by "the high contracting parties" that "Check Nights" should be given up, and that "Boating Bills" should be conceded instead thereof. Similarly, soon afterwards it was agreed that in consideration of a debauch known as "Oppidan Dinner" being discontinued the Eight should be allowed to take part at Henley Regatta. Of course the "time-honoured old customs" were not parted with, even upon terms, with general acquiescence; but owing to the admirable policy of the Head Master and his advisers, the only grievance of the malcontents was with their own Captain, who they chose to consider had sold them, but who in truth had most sensibly thrown all his influence on the side of the authorities in exchange for very favourable terms while they were to be had.

Rather more than a mile above Boveney is Surly, a place whose name is as familiar to the present generation as " Salt Hill " was to the last, from its being the destination of the aquatic Procession on the 4th of June, which has come into more prominent notice since the abolition of " Montem." Surly Hall is a well-conducted river-side inn, at which boys who have rowed so far are allowed to refresh. Just beyond it is "The Willows," the place of Mr. Eykyn, M.P. for Windsor, with a charming lawn, part of which may be noticed in our etching, sloping down to the water. In the bay formed here is one of the deepest pools—if not the deepest—on the Thames. How deep that hole is we are afraid to say, for whatever figure we stop at the Surly fishermen will assuredly go beyond us. The procession of " the Boats " at the Regatta of the 4th of June stops about a quarter of a mile short of Surly Hall, and there the crews in their fancy dresses disembark at a temporary enclosure, in which the *al-fresco* supper takes place. This annual fête is a good example of the extent to which by the Eton system the boys are left by the authorities to manage things for themselves. Though there are no " prefects," and the monitorial power does not exist as it is understood elsewhere, there is no school where so much confidence is reposed in boys in influential positions as at Eton, or where the authorities interfere so little out of school. The system of government, too, which by immemorial custom exists among the boys themselves is somewhat peculiar. There are no such things as Committees, or divided responsibility. At the head of each department is an autocrat who is responsible only to the public opinion of the " miniature state." Thus it is that the Fourth of June Regatta is managed solely and entirely by the Captain of the Oppidans. He has to estimate the cost, which is about £200,* and to raise the money by a poll-tax varying in proportion to grade in school ; he is then responsible for all the arrangements, the selection of tradesmen, the contracts that are made with them,

---

* When Election Saturday was also observed, about £350 was required.

SURLY
HALL
B. HARRIS

and payment of the accounts. He is guided in his duties by the records of his predecessors, but his discretion in the matter is subjected to no magisterial control. It is not so very many years since the 4th of June Regatta was ignored altogether by the Masters; for as the river was then "out of bounds," and in theory the boys were always within the limits of College, the Masters were obliged to feign ignorance of what was going on; and the story is told that William IV., desirous of putting an end to this absurdity, invited Dr. Keate to dine with him on the 4th of June, and having proposed after dinner that they should go for a drive "to a place the Doctor had never been at before," took the perplexed Head Master to the Brocas during the procession of Boats. Soon afterwards the river was declared to be "in bounds," and at the same time, upon the usual give-and-take principle, regulations were made, and boys who could not swim were absolutely, instead of nominally, forbidden to boat. Nevertheless the management of the Regatta remained with the boys; for that was in accordance with the general system, of which it is cited as an example. The Captains of the School, Oppidans, Boats, and Eleven, the Captains of Houses, and many others, have confidence reposed in them, with its accompanying responsibilities, to a very large extent, the natural effect of which is to enlist all the influential boys upon the side of "order," and at the same time not only to develop their self-respect and in its train all other right feelings, but also by obviating the necessity for constant magisterial interference and espionage to raise the tone of the whole school and create that manly and straightforward spirit in which English public school boys so immeasurably excel those of the continent. For what is here said of Eton is of course true in varying degrees of all our great schools. The principle is the same throughout; and it is one of which the Great Duke expressed his admiration by saying that "the Battle of Waterloo was won in the Eton Playing Fields;" and which more recently drew from Montalembert the following eloquent tribute to its merits. Speaking of the Indian Mutiny, and

H

citing the names of the heroes who shone in it, he said:* "They do honour to the human race; but it is not only such names, great beyond comparison, it is the bearing in every respect of this handful of Englishmen surprised in the midst of peace and prosperity by the most frightful and most unforeseen of catastrophes. Not one of them shrank or trembled; all, military and civilians, young and old, generals and soldiers resisted, fought, and perished with a coolness and intrepidity which never faltered. It is in this circumstance that shines out the immense value of public education, which invites the Englishman from his youth to make use of his strength and his liberty, to associate, resist, fear nothing, be astonished at nothing, and to save himself by his own sole exertions from every sore strait in life."

While the author has digressed to attempt a slight "sketch" of the Eton method of government, his partner has completed a "sketch" of the Thames at WATER OAKLEY, a spot about a mile above Surly, and as far below Monkey Island, whose poplars appear away on the right. In the left-hand corner of the picture two pleasant river-side properties meet—Oakley Court, built a few years back by Mr. Hall Saye and recently purchased by Lord Otho Fitzgerald; and Down Place (Mrs. Harford's), where the "Kit-Kat Club" was started by Jacob Tonson the bookseller, and its members occasionally enjoyed "the feast of reason and the flow of soul." The straight reach of water in front has been used of late years—in preference to the course lower down—for the "Trial Eights," a race which has been substituted for the time-honoured contests between "Dames and Tutors" and "Two sides of College." MONKEY ISLAND is a favourite resort of Eton aquatics, though as it is five miles from Windsor Bridge, and the stream in the last mile is of great strength, their visits are necessarily of limited duration. The small Hotel there was built as a fishing-lodge by a Duke of Marlborough at the end of last century, and the place obtains its designation from the fact that

---

* Quoted in Smiles' "Self-Help."

in one of the rooms of this house the walls are painted with monkeys dressed like men, and engaged in various sports, in imitation of similar wall-painting at the palace of Chantilly in the apartments which the unfortunate Duc d'Enghien occupied in his youth. The situation of " Monkey " is marked far and wide by several lofty poplars which grow there. Our etching is taken from Amerden Bank, a farm house a few hundred yards higher up, and just below Bray Lock ; and we also give typographs of

MONKEY ISLAND—LANDING PLACE.

the Landing-place—beneath four stately poplars which the exigencies of our space have cut very short—and of an old Billiard Room which stands apart from the Monkey House.

This part of the river was the scene of the second eight-oared race rowed between Eton and Westminster, which took place in May, 1831, the course being from Maidenhead Bridge round Monkey Island and back, a distance of about five miles. Eton led throughout, and avoiding a collision at the turning point, ultimately won by a quarter of a mile, the race having taken about forty-five minutes to accomplish. The sporting account of the period says that a " vast assemblage " lined the towing-path, and that " it would be in vain to attempt to describe the feeling that was manifested at the result of the match." Of the first eight Eton and Westminster races, each school won four; Eton won the ninth match in 1847, and then the race was discontinued till 1860. On its revival, Eton having won four times running, and boating having been altogether driven away from the river at Westminster by the steamers and the Thames Embankment, the race was again and (in all probability) finally

BILLIARD ROOM.

discontinued. It is scarcely necessary to observe that when the race was rowed at Monkey, Bray Lock was not in existence. It was constructed a few years afterwards to obviate the shallowness and rapidity of the stream at that point, but the fall in the lock is slight, and at seasons when the river is full the gates are frequently left open. Of course we cannot pass BRAY without the remark that this is where " The Vicar of Bray " resided ; cela va sans dire,—but unfortunately the parish records do not confirm the tradition of that versatile individual's existence. Fuller in his "Worthies of England," published in 1661, speaks of him as having undergone his several " conversions " in the reigns of

Monkey Island
1873

Henry VIII. and his three successors, so that the song placing him in the Stewart period is at the least guilty of a slight anachronism, and is no doubt religiously proscribed in the society of those virtuous historians who were recently goaded to fury by the members of an Oxford College taking advantage of their traditional " millenary " to have a festive gathering. In Bray Church is a monument to a gentleman of whom it is stated that " next to treason he hated debt," which after all may not be saying much for his loyalty.

BRAY LOCK.

About a mile above Bray the main line of the Great Western Railway is carried over the Thames at Taplow by a remarkable bridge, one of the many bold achievements of Brunel, that daring engineer whose soaring genius never permitted him to condescend to the common-place or to keep in a path that had been cleared by others. The two main arches of the bridge are the largest and flattest *brick* arches in the world, each being a semi-ellipse of 128 feet span and 24 feet rise. The river is nearly 300 feet wide at this point, and advantage is taken of an island in mid-stream on which to rest the centre pier. The structure is so graceful that, as a rare exception to railway works, it is an ornament instead of an eyesore even amidst the natural charms of the valley of the Thames. A few hundred yards beyond we reach MAIDENHEAD BRIDGE, where the old coach road to the West of England crosses the river. It is as great a contrast to its modern neighbour as well could be, but is one of the most picturesque bridges by which man has defeated the noble river which would obstruct his free passage;—*free* passage we have written, momentarily oblivious of the toll that is still levied in primæval fashion; nevertheless, kind reader (if there be one still in our company), let it pass. Maidenhead derives its name, according to Leland

and others, from a " large wharf "—" Magne Hithe "—which formerly existed there for the purposes of the timber trade; but as we should be sorry to hurt the feelings of those who see in the name a memorial of the decapitation of some saintly virgin, we forbear to express any personal opinion on the subject. We have now reached the outside limit which an Eton boy can possibly attain without leave of absence, and must therefore turn back to College. We will, however, take the high road to Slough, instead of the direct cross-road by Dorney, in order to pass Salt Hill and get a sketch, without which no account of Eton could be considered in any way complete.

V.

SALT HILL.

SALT HILL is a mere mound situated near Slough, close to the London and Bath road, and distant about two miles from Eton College, with which its name must ever be inseparably connected on account of the existence for probably four centuries of the custom called "Montem." Of course everybody knows that this consisted in a fancy-dress procession to the Hill (ad "Montem"), and that the latter derived its name from the term applied by the boys to the money collected from the spectators to defray some of the expenses of the day and to make a purse for the Captain of the School on his going up to the University. What nobody knows is how and when this custom originated and what it all meant.

It is generally agreed that in some shape or other the ceremony was coeval with the College, and the most plausible hypothesis seems to be that it was the procession of the "Boy Bishop." Originally it took place on St. Nicholas' day, and it was certainly customary at Salisbury and elsewhere to give the mock dignity of "bishop" to a boy on that day; and there is no doubt that at Montem in last century one boy was dressed in clerical costume and read certain Latin prayers. A Mr. Cole of King's College, in a note to some MSS. he gave to the British Museum early in the present century, asserts that a certain Bishop Blythe, who deceased in 1530, left several ornaments for the dress of "the boy bishop;" but as that prelate's will is lost, it is not possible either to confirm or contradict the statement of Mr. Cole. At an early period Montem day was changed to 2nd February, and took place every other year only; and Dr. Barnard had a good nibble at the institution, for in his time it was made triennial, and

"several of its abuses retrenched;" but on the other hand the
day was changed from the winter to Whit-Tuesday.   Whatever
its origin, the procession came to be of a military character; the
second Boy in the school led with the title of Marshal, then came
the Captain with eight Lower Boys in attendance, and the third
in rank brought up the rear as Lieutenant.   Another was Ensign,

SALT HILL.

and carried the colours, which were emblazoned with the motto
"Pro more et Monte."   It is supposed that the collection of
money for "salt" came from an ancient practice among the friars
of selling consecrated salt.   It is certainly possible that the boys
would take such a hint, and endeavour to raise an honest penny
in the same way.   The salt-bearers were gorgeously attired, and
collected from all persons present, "even from passengers travel-
ling the road."   A considerable sum was obtained in this way,

but the greater part went to defray the expenses, as the Captain entertained the whole school at Salt Hill, and from all accounts with too little stint.

The last Montem took place on May 28, 1844. The time-honoured ceremony was abolished in 1847, Provost Hodgson being the man who dared its destruction, and by so doing secured for himself rather more than the usual amount of odium and abuse dealt out to reformers by their contemporaries. We venture to think that if he had spared his pains, time would have done the work for him, as it is scarcely conceivable—the Lord Mayor's Show notwithstanding—that the mummery would have retained its popularity in the present day when the rage for Athletic exhibitions is ousting everything of the kind. There was of course a prodigious outcry at Mr. Hodgson's arbitrary edict. Two large meetings of old Etonians were held in London, including several noble lords and M.P.'s, a Vice Chancellor of England, a Vice Admiral, and a venerable clergyman, to protest against the abolition, denounce the Provost, and petition the Crown to interfere. A letter was read from Mr. Hodgson, in which he spoke of the ceremony as "a splendid show," but said that it had "immoral tendencies," and caused "great indulgence and extravagance;" that the railway would "cause an influx of objectionable characters;" and that "the Captain in a great number of instances had been injured rather than benefited by the collection." The *Times'* report relates that the last statement was met with "an indignant denial from several present," and that the allusion to the "immoral tendencies" was "greeted with shouts of derision." A memorial to the Queen received upwards of 300 signatures on the spot, but the Crown "saw no grounds for interference." On 25th May (Whit-Tuesday), the day on which the procession would have taken place, disturbances were expected at Eton ; but "nothing occurred beyond a strong muster of old and young Etonians at Salt Hill, adorned with black crape." Thus the defunct ceremony received decent obsequies.

Another ancient Eton custom long since abolished was that of "hunting the ram," which took place in " Election week," the participators in " the pastime " being mounted, as appears from the following letter, which we have had opportunities of seeing, and which may be of interest as a specimen of an Eton boy's letter home at that period :—

"Etone, ye 21st July, 1687.

" Honored Sir—This is to acquaent you that the electione being near att hand, which is our usuall vacation from business and with your leave a time appointed for home enjoyments, and prosuming opon an old custome that you will be pleased to grant this, I further request you to send ye horses for us, that they may be here tomorrow about noon which will make our journey far more pleasant and att ye least give us ye satisfaction of seeing ye ram die here as is according to custome. I hope you will not think this my request unreasonablee and therefore will gratifie me, giving my duty to my honoured mother and my service to my cousen, and my kind love to my brothers and sisters, who am, sir, youre most dutefull son,   EDWARD WOOD."

(Addressed) " For my honoured father, Mr. Wood,
living at Littleton."

With this short notice of the ancient customs of the place we must reluctantly conclude our " Sketches of Eton."

WATSON AND HAZELL, Printers, London and Aylesbury.